# From Nun to Mom

## And More

## A Poetic Collection with Stories

### by
### Betty J. Osowski

Edited by Hella Buchheim
Cover Design by Deborah McMahon
Page Design & Layout by Linda Coffin

Personal Histories Publishing
Minneapolis, MN
PO Box 4095
Hopkins, MN 55343


Copyright ©2009
ISBN # 978-0-9790731-3-7
0-9790731-3-8

# Contents

| POEM / STORY | PAGE |
| --- | --- |

# Foreword

This spring, 2008, I read to my daughter Ann one of the poems I wrote about her at the time she chose not to connect with me. Obviously it was a poem expressing my sadness because she was not letting me get close to her. She wanted to hear some of my other poems and what inspired me to write them. It seemed like I was exposing her to a "me" that she did not yet know. After going through several poems, she said, "Mom, you have to publish these." Surprised by her response I replied, "Ann, some of these poems are very good, but only some." Her response was, "Next to the poem you have to write the story that inspired you. We all want to hear stories that in some way touch our human experiences, whether joyful or painful, hopeful or hopeless."

This encounter led me to write the story of my life, selecting experiences, events, relationships, and decisions that directed and influenced "who I am, where I am, and how I am today," the sum total of me, yet always a person in process. Most of the poems and the stories: *A Braided Family* and *A Young Girl's Memories Farm and Family* were written in the late nineteen nineties. The other poems and stories in my collection were written more recently.

Someday maybe a great-grandchild will say, "I was born in America because my great-grandmother Betty adopted my grandmother Ruth, and brought her from Korea to America. What kind of a woman was my great-grandmother?"

# Acknowledgments

My first words of gratitude and respect go to my maternal great grandparents Andrew and Josephine Yach who came to America from Poland in 1866, and my paternal grandparents John and Veronica Osowski who came to America from Poland in 1885. Who I am, that I am, and where I am is the result of the daring decision they made to leave the oppression they were experiencing in their motherland to come to this land of freedom, America. Thank you!

Mother and Dad, beloved brothers Leonard and Elmer, you were my first family and friends that showed me how to love and to be loved. Thank you!

Bóg zapłac, (may God reward you) Sisters of St. Joseph, Third Order of St. Francis. You were my teachers from Grade One through Grade twelve. You inspired me to aspire to a meaningful life of service. It was a privilege to be a member of your religious family for almost one third of my life. Thank you!

I have enjoyed each pupil I taught in my years of teaching in Catholic Schools. Wherever you are today, I hope spirituality is one of your uncompromising values.

To the wonderful people I have come to know in my work in religious education and formation: Resurrection Parish in Green Bay, Wisconsin; St. Peter's Parish in North St. Paul, Minnesota; St. William Parish in Fridley, Minnesota; Guardian Angels Parish in Oakdale, Minnesota, you have and continue to strengthen me in my journey of faith. Thank You!

I am eternally indebted to a few very close special friends on whom I call or visit in times of tears, laughter and in between, Jackie, Mary, and Ray and Eileen.

My sister-in-law, Jacqueline Osowski, I thank you for sixty years of friendship. It's wonderful sharing each other's poetry when we get together.

Imagine what profound poems we will experience in eternal life. There has to be poetry and music there, wouldn't you think?

Sister Mary Nolan, Sister of Charity, BVM, our thirty-five years of friendship is a gift. We continue to call one another to the authenticity of our distinctive life styles and avocations. Thank you!

Raymond and Eileen Muetzel, I perhaps have leaned the most on your love, support, generosity and wisdom since leaving the convent and coming to St. Peter's Parish. You can't even imagine what blessings I will send your way to you and your family if I enter eternity before you. Thank you!

In closing I need to say, my most valued relationships are with my daughters Ruth, Ann, Teresa, Mary, and my grandchildren. I cherish all of our family memories. I look forward to the treasured time I will continue to have with those with whom I am connected, and I wait with deep longing for others to re-connect.

# Introduction

We have one life to live on this beautiful planet earth, and we have the privilege and responsibility to live that life meaningfully for ourselves, for others and for the world. Discerning that purposeful life takes interesting paths influenced by many factors, some of which are – our family of origin and ancestry, significant relationships, the desires of our heart, mind and gut, poverty, hunger, dire needs in the world and cultural, educational and religious experiences.

In this book I highlight my unique path and some of the influences that helped direct me in experiencing joy and fulfillment in my seventy-eight years of life. Hopefully I continue to discern new paths and embrace the courage to walk a new path if I hear the call.

I remember as a young child singing the hymn *Hail Holy Queen*. In this song earth is described as a "valley of tears." A young child usually sees beauty and wonder in the world. It's when the child enters the teen world and the adult world that personal pain and the pain in the world is seen and felt. In our journey of life we experience many emotions.

I have met and interacted with tens of thousands of adults. I would have to probe my memory to find one adult who has not experienced deep pain in his or her life. Most of us also have experienced joys and consolations and we breezed through them. But what do we do with pain?

I am learning to walk with pain and not let it make me bitter, hopeless or stagnant. In this process I can honestly say I wouldn't trade a memory or event in my life, happy or sad, joyful or painful, because they make me the person I am today, very blessed, very grateful and hopefully more compassionate.

# The Pail and the Dipper

As a small child
I remember entering
my grandparent's house on the farm
and pausing to drink water
from the pail and the dipper
on the table by the door.

It seemed like an early cocktail
teasing my appetite for
the main course that would follow
later that day.

The men played cards
the women shared stories
and the cousins meandered
all over the farm, until

the feast of produce
from the land and
the pies baked in the wood-burning stove

sent us
on our way home
loved and fed,
and

it all started
with the pail
and the dipper
on the table
by the door.

# A Young Girl's Memories of Farm and Family

## I. Babusia

I was seven years old when my parents left me at Grandma Josephine's farm for my first summer vacation. She always sat in her big oak rocker across from the front door, anticipating company. Our family usually came for a visit on Sunday afternoons. My brothers and I would join the cousins exploring the farm and it's potentially mischevous adventures, while the grown-ups gathered around a rather well worn kitchen table and played cards.

I heard my dad's new Ford leave the farmyard. Dziadzia went to the barn. I sat in a maroon chair diagonally across from Babusia's rocker, wondering what she and I would do. She spoke Polish. My Polish vocabulary was limited to the Sign of the Cross, the Our Father and the Hail Mary.

Then a miraculous "Helen Keller event" took place. A fly flew from her rocker to my chair. She pointed to the winged insect and said, "Mucha!" My eyes widened and I shouted, "Fly!" At that moment we not only connected with words, but our grandmother granddaughter relationship was born. Before the week was over I recognized the meaning of Polish phrases like, "sweep the floor," "pump water," and "get some strawberries." She in turn knew the meaning of the English words, "I love you" and "give me a kiss."

After that week I was envious when Babusia played pinochle with the adults on Sunday afternoons. Not only did I want to learn more Polish, I really wanted to know her better, my grandmother Josephine.

# II. Dziadzia

My grandfather was a kind soft-spoken man, actually a silent man when Babusia raised her voice. He could speak some English so we were friends from the beginning. He'd call me "his little summer farmer" because I would spend a week each summer at the maternal homestead.

In the middle of the week he'd crave brandy and friends and he took me with him to the General Store near Sacred Heart Church in Polonia, Wisconsin, a few miles from the farm. I'd play with the store owner's children while grandpa had a few drinks at the bar talking in Polish about the weather and the crops. He always bought me a bag of pink and white mints, the kind that looked like fat 3D nickels. I hated them but I never told him.

On Sunday afternoons in winter we would ski down the hills on homemade skis that had a strap to hold our boots. In the evening we played in-house games and breathed in the familiar smell of smoke and beer from the gang in the kitchen. Even when it snowed hard, someone from the card table would always say, "Just one more game." More than a few times my brothers and I sat in the back seat of the car curled up under the buffalo skin blanket given to us from our other grandpa, while Dziadzia and the horses pulled our car out of the snowdrift piled up from a day of heavy snowing. Tired and cold we could never figure out why someone would always say, "Just one more game."

# III. Jordan River

The farm was thirteen miles from my home in Stevens Point. Half way there we would cross the Jordan River, a large sprawling body of water on both sides of Highway 66. On very hot humid days we'd stop for a short swim on the way to the farm. My dad and brothers swam in a spot around the bend. I had to stay with my mother and wade in shallow water. I became a good swimmer by the age of ten and I wanted to join the male component of my family. It was then that I found out why I was restricted from swimming around the bend; the male component swam in the nude.

Leaving the farm late Sunday evenings we had to cross the Jordan River again. Remembering my dad's mix of pinochle, brandy and beer, I lowered my head between my knees, closed my eyes and prayed until the river was behind us. To this day my deepest fear is plunging into a body of water in a car.

# IV. My Godparents

My mother had eight sisters and three brothers. Her oldest sister Veronie and Veronie's husband Joe were my godparents. I loved them almost as much as my parents. They owned a farm three miles from the homestead where my mother was born.

Aunt Veronie had five miscarriages and stillborn births before she finally gave birth to a healthy son, Donnie. Each time she lost a baby she'd sew more dresses for me. One day I counted thirty dresses in my closet on 725 Portage Street.

Uncle Joe was the kindest man I knew. I called him my "damn uncle" because he couldn't talk for one minute without using the word "damn." It was never meant to be mean, just to make a point.

I cherished my week in summer on their farm and stretched each waking hour. I can't tell you what I loved the most: the three people in this family, the incredible experiences of each day or the scrumptious meals produced from the land and prepared by the greatest cook in the world. Don't tell my mother the latter.

Late afternoons I could hear my Uncle Joe calling, "Come boss, come boss," and the cows with dripping udders would waddle slowly from the ravished meadow to the barn. Each of my Uncle's cows had a name and he swore that the name fit the cow's "cow-ality." My Uncle and his hired man sat on three legged stools and milked each cow by hand. If I got close to the cow he was milking he'd turn that teat and squirt me in the face with warm unpasteurized milk… yek!

While I was sleeping the cows were milked again early in the morning and sent to pasture. After the milking my Uncle would sneak into my bedroom and tickle me under the nose with a wet weed. The predicted response ensued, the wiggling and wrinkling of the skin under my nose, followed by a movement of my fingers to chase the presumed fly, and finally, the opening of my eyes and mouth admitting, "He did it again, my damn uncle."

# V. Donnie

Of the forty-one first cousins on my mother's side of the family Donnie was my favorite. When I was younger he treated me nicer than my brothers did, probably because he had no siblings, or maybe, because he liked me. At ages seven and nine we promised to marry each other – at ten and twelve we were deadly enemies.

After evening chores he'd chase me with a canning jar of muddy water. Sometimes I'd run more than a half mile rather than give him the satisfaction of throwing the muck in my face. Once he chased me into a six-foot tall cornfield holding a garter snake in his hand. I wanted to despise him but he was too good-looking.

Sometimes we would climb on top of the barn stalls and jump on the heifers. They'd go berserk and run in circles trying to shake us off. The day my damn uncle saw cowpat stains on our faded overalls was the last day we rode the heifers.

When Donnie was twelve years old he was forced to take a picture with me wearing my First Communion dress. We were directed to stand against the side of the house that had morning glory vines twining up the wall. Just a split second before the click of the camera Donnie managed to pull a vine in front of him and it covered his whole face. It's my favorite picture of us.

Years later I entered the convent. Donnie married Alice.

# VI. My Paternal Grandparents

My dad's mother Veronica died two years before I was born. I know little about her life, but one story seems to capture her spirit. She bought the first and only family car. Each Sunday she drove the children to St. Mary's Church in Toran, Wisconsin. Grandpa walked. What a gutsy Grandma!

Grandpa John was born in Poland in 1851. I have two existential questions to ask him when we meet in eternity. "Why did you leave Poland? Why did you choose to settle in central Wisconsin?" That I am, who I am, and where I am is the result of the responses to these questions.

My father was the second youngest of eleven surviving brothers and sisters. I never met all of them, and knew only some of my fifty-nine paternal cousins. The mystery of why this family was so disconnected saddens me to this day. If it wasn't for the love and affection of my maternal relatives, "family" would be just a word in the dictionary.

Dad visited Grandpa John every month. I was usually afraid to go see him. His messy beard, white kinky hair and loud rough voice frightened me. I did however, force myself to go at least twice a year because he opened a finger smeared cigar box and handed me a new dollar bill each time I visited.

I was fourteen years old when grandpa died. I will never forget his wake in the family living room. The house was thick with people, smoke, beer, stories and laughter. I rather liked it.

## VII. Picking

As a young girl I couldn't decide whether picking was work or pleasure. In time I concluded that picking was work that produced pleasure.

Twice a day the warm white and tan eggs had to be picked from the chicken coop.

Every day the ripe red apples and purple blue plums had to be picked from the ground in the orchard.

On Sunday Babusia asked me to pick pink and yellow slightly opened rosebuds from the rose garden.

My favorite picking place was in the woods. I still can see myself picking –

sky-blue blueberries,
deep black blackberries,
lightly tanned mushrooms,
yellowish brown hazelnuts –

each in due season.

Undoubtedly the biggest picking was from the garden –

spring green peas,
shy red raspberries,
proud red strawberries and tomatoes,

green cucumbers, celery and kohlrabi,
mature broccoli and cauliflower,
very orange carrots and pumpkins,
mellow zucchini and sour rhubarb,
golden gold corn and new white potatoes.

Fortunately, the produce didn't ripen at the same time. I was so glad when the first snowfall came because there was no more picking for a long time.

## VIII. The Farmhouse

To a small child from the city the farmhouse looked like an enormous mansion. It was an attractive redbrick house with a white trim and a frontal porch that wrapped around the east and south side of the house.

The main entrance to the house was on the west side. Often Dziadzia sat on the hand carved glider and rocked like a metronome set at adagio. When our family of five arrived I was usually the first to enter the house. "Hi Babusia and Dziadzia." Then I would drink a full dipper of well water from the pail on a small table near the door. It represented hospitality to me, like the gospel stories saying they either did or didn't wash the feet of those who came to eat. Well, my grandparents did.

The adults always gathered around the kitchen table and rarely moved to the parlors unless many relatives arrived at the same time. Aunts and uncles came unannounced but never unexpected. If the group was large the women visited in the first parlor while the men played cards in the kitchen.

The second parlor, which I called the fancy parlor had quaint furniture, an antiquated pump organ and an old player piano. On very rainy or snowy days the cousins would sit or stand around the piano to sing and jazz up the golden olden tunes. Of the over fifty piano rolls, "Among My Souvenirs" was my favorite.

By four o'clock in the afternoon appetizing smells of fresh meat fried with onions, and cooked vegetables hovered over the wood-burning stove in the kitchen, then finally wafted to the other thirteen rooms in the house. We feasted from the heaping platters and bowls in the center of the table, and it is my unscientific observation that deserts played an important part in Polish menus.

Sometimes in the evening in winter on very frigid days we'd play hide-and-seek in the dark bedrooms and closets upstairs. Because I was usually the only girl cousin they played Frankenstein pranks on me. I wanted to hate boys but if I did I would have had a lonely childhood.

Around the age of fourteen my peers and our activities became more important than my cousins and the farm. Summer vacations stopped and I visited the farm only a few times a year on Sunday afternoons.

The homestead now belongs to my uncle's great grandson who hopes to one day hand it on to his son. Occasionally I revisit the farm in the treasury of memories etched in my heart. I can see, feel, hear, smell and taste some of the happiest and most fulfilling experiences of my childhood.

# HAPPY MOTHER'S DAY

### From Teresa Ann to Mom, May 9, 1999

Some of my childhood memories are…
>  playing board games
>  playing catch out in the back yard
>  visiting family and friends

I enjoyed doing those things with you because…
>  We were together. It was fun
>  being a kid and not worrying
>  about being in charge (like I was
>  before I came to live with you).

I will always remember when…
>  You praised me for doing a good
>  job. We did things together as a
>  family and just you and I. You always
>  took time to listen to me. When you
>  burned cabbage rolls in the oven to
>  bring me to the hospital when I
>  broke my leg.

I admire you for many reasons…
>  your unconditional love
>  your smile
>  how generous you are
>  taking time to listen
>  your faith in God
>  knowing you're always there for me
>  all your work with foster children

I am so grateful that you…
>  taught me to swim, ride a bike,
>  bat ball, all the childhood games
>  I didn't learn before, thanks

I'm proud of you for many things…
>  being a great foster and adoptive mom,
>  and all your church work

I've learned many things from you…
> how to be patient
> how to help others
> how to love and show love
> how to give and not always
> take

My favorite memory is…
> any Christmas from the first
> when I was ten until now at
> the age of thirty

My favorite Polish tradition is…
> breaking bread with each
> other at Christmas because
> it's a chance to wish a loved
> one something special for the
> New Year.

I'll always treasure…
> our time together, holidays,
> camping, relatives, friends
> going on vacations, the day
> you adopted Mary and I and
> gave us your name and family

> **Why did you…**
> **become a nun and then a**
> **mom?**

> Even though I didn't
> always show it, and some-
> times I didn't say it – I love
> you mom! Thank you for
> being my mom. You are my
> mom in all the ways that
> count and matter! Love,

**Terri Ann Rose**

# A Braided Family

In my home of origin at 725 Portage Street, there were two small bedrooms on the second floor separated by a narrow hallway leading to a bathroom. My bedroom had two half windows facing the northern sky, and my two brothers shared a bedroom on the south side of the house. I went to bed most nights feeling alone as the laughter from my brothers' room seeped through my closed door. I wanted a sister, someone who would be there with me in a way that brothers couldn't. I was very close to the God of the northern sky and often I would rest my arms on the window sill while my eyes reached the stars and my heart prayed, "It's me again, Lord, asking for a sister."

For years I asked my parents to have another child. When I was nine years old they told me my mother had been very ill giving birth to me and they decided not to have more children. One day I asked my mother, "Why don't you adopt a child so that I can have a sister?" Without hesitation my mother replied, "I could never love another person's child like my own."

When I was forty-six years old I took someone else's child into my home, into my life. At noon, February 16, 1976, a sad and puzzled seven and a half year old Thai-Korean girl was brought to my door by her social worker. For over two years I had been approved by Catholic Charities in Saint Paul, Minnesota, for the adoption of an eight-year old girl still residing in an orphanage in Seoul, Korea. The social worker that had approved my home for the adoption knew that I had hoped to adopt two girls, and when the adoption of this child failed, I was overwhelmed at the surprise and short notice of her placement into my home.

When I first saw "my" child I wanted to pick her up into my arms and hug her lovingly, but the fear and distrust in her eyes told me that "hugs and kisses" would come much later. She greeted me by my first name Betty. Her adoptive family named her Kyann. I asked her if I could give her a new name because she would be living in a new family. This was a suggestion given to me by her social worker. She agreed and accepted the name Ann Mary. As we unpacked her belongings I noticed a calendar. Paging through the calendar I saw that she had crossed out the birthdays of the members of her adoptive family. She informed me she wanted two birthdays in this family so I marked her birthday again and the date of her arrival, indeed, a new "birth" day. She wanted me to write the birthdays of the members of our family. I added relatives and friends so she wouldn't think there were only two of us in the newly formed family.

That afternoon she spent several hours sliding down the snow hills with my friends' children. They referred to me as her "mom" and by late afternoon she began calling me "mom". In the evening as we gathered at the supper table she realized and said, "There only two people in our family." I pointed to the picture on the table of her sister in Korea and said, "No, three." Ruth will soon be coming from Korea to join our family. She replied, "Then how many after that, five, ten?" I laughed at her question and had no idea it would be a forecast of years to come when I would indeed foster over thirty-five children through the course of almost two decades.

I waited long for that special night in my life when I would rock my very own daughter to sleep. Instead, Ann cried desperately from the bedroom, "Go away. I no be happy until you take me to other family." I sat on the floor by the door tasting her pain in the salt of my tears until her last whimper led her into a deep sleep.

Morning came, the tears on her pillow had long dried, and Ann began the task of coloring an ABC book. Each morning she colored one or two pages. We talked, laughed, and played, filling her day and mind with new memories. School was her best attraction and distraction from dwelling on the trauma of another uprooting. Ann in her young seven and a half years of life had been uprooted three times; first, from her biological mother who formed and nurtured her; second, from the orphanage in Korea where she was happy; and third, from the family who brought her from Korea to America and now chose to give her up. Ann also had three name changes.

Three months after Ann was placed with me we stood at a Northwest Airlines gate waiting for Ruth's plane to arrive. It took almost two years to receive a visa to come to America to a single parent family. Then, at 8:15 pm on May 27, 1976, this strikingly beautiful and frightened child walked into the airport with her escort. I knelt beside her saying, "Mama and Ruth" and gently hugged her as tears flowed from my face to her cheeks. She showed no emotion. Her escort said she threw up several times enroute. It wasn't until we reached home and she recognized everything in our living room and her bedroom. She then realized I was her mother and she was home. At the airport I must have looked different from the pictures she received two years previously. She jumped into my arms and hugged me with all the strength her scrawny arms could release. Bonding that began thousands of miles away and kissing pictures at night, now was incarnate. The evening of celebration began. Friends, gifts, tears, hugs, and Korean bows continued long into the night. Ruth loved to sing and we experienced a portion of her remarkable repertoire of songs always accompanied by rhythmic gestures or dance steps.

I have never known the joyful experience of giving birth and raising my own biological children, but my delight at being mother to these two girls was beyond comprehension. For years I prayed the last verse of Psalm 113, and hoped it would one day be a reality in my life:

*He has blessed the barren woman with a home*
*and made her the joyful mother of children.*

My desire to be a parent was instinctual. At age six when asked by my teacher, "What do you want to be when you are an adult?" My response was, "A Sister and a mother of ten children." I then learned that I couldn't be both. It was explained to me that being a Sister in the Roman Catholic tradition meant not having children of my own. At sixteen and a half the desire to commit myself to God as a religious Sister was stronger than my desire for children.

I enjoyed twenty-four fulfilling years in a religious community. Indeed, my life was dedicated to children through the teaching profession. Yet, I longed for a family of my own. Two years after I left the community I became acquainted with Kathy and Ron, who later became Ann's godparents. They were waiting for a son from Korea and discovered that their social worker had placed two Korean brothers with a single woman. Agencies in the mid-seventies were just looking into single parent adoption, especially for foreign-born children and foster children. Shortly after hearing of this case I began my home study with the intent of adopting a Korean girl. God's plan was greater than my expectation. Ruth was my desired child. Ann was God's surprise child.

For two years we were a family of three. Ann had been in America for one year before coming to live with me and the American language had rapidly replaced her Korean language. Ruth's English consisted of two words, "Mama, banana." As both of the girls improved their knowledge and use of the language, we began to share our stories, our histories. We had come from three very different worlds.

Ann was brought to an orphanage in Kunsan, Korea, when she was one month old. She remained there until she came to the United States at age six and a half. Unlike Ruth's sad experiences, Ann always spoke lovingly about her early childhood years. A caring Christian couple served as Directors of the orphanage. Their biological children assisted them in the care of the orphans. Ann had a special fondness for one of their daughters whom she called "Uhnnee," meaning older sister. Uhnnee and "Uhmma," the orphanage mother and Director, were the most significant people in Ann's early childhood. Because they loved and affirmed her she came to the United States with the ability to bond to caring adults.

Unfortunately, the family who adopted her did not provide the nurturing environment needed for her continued development. Ann remembered being deprived of her meals many times as punishment for some unacceptable behavior. She was sent to her room for extended periods of time. She spoke of verbal abuse from her mother and her two siblings. She did receive care and concern from her adoptive father. Many factors contributed to this failed adoption, some of which were the language barrier, cultural adjustment difficulties, unreasonable parental expectations of Ann, and marital problems. When Ann came into my life she carried the pain and guilt of a twofold rejection, namely, that of her biological parents and her American adoptive parents. Would the pain ever go away?

Ruth was raised in an orphanage in Seoul, Korea. She loved the United States from the moment she stepped off the airplane. After learning the meaning of the word beautiful, for months she said, "Beautiful America" each time we took a drive in the car. What Ruth wanted more than anything else in the whole world was to have her very own mother. She felt safe and secure in my presence, and she experienced fear and frustration when I had to leave her with others because of work. As she learned the appropriate English words to describe the inhuman forms of abuse she experienced in the orphanage, she proceeded to relate incident after incident with deep pain and anger. We cried together as I held and comforted her. Most of her anger was turned inwards and the rage was manifested in periodic serious temper tantrums. She spoke of wanting to go back to Korea someday to kill those who abused her. Would the pain ever go away?

I was born in 1930 in the city of Stevens Point, Wisconsin. We were a family of five. Some of the happiest memories of my childhood were related to seasonal activities, camping, swimming, fishing, and skiing. My grandparents and relatives lived in nearby rural communities. I welcomed the opportunity to spend Sundays at the farm and a week or two in the summer.

I have always felt a close affinity with nature and my seasonal and rural experiences nurtured this relationship. The repetitive image of vast farm fields frozen with snow awaiting the faithful appearance of my grandfather each spring to plow and to plant, taught me early about the stages of life, about dying and rising within myself, creation, family life, and the communities to which I belong. Later in some of the difficult periods in my daughters' adolescence I would recall the image of a vast farm field frozen with snow and remember that spring and new life will follow.

Our three very different worlds of heritage, environment and life styles braided, as we set out to become a family. While we called ourselves a family, in reality this did not happen until the bonding and memory making processes were long underway. A family derives its unique identity from its values ritualized in shared experiences then replayed in memory. Our family mandala completed its outer circle when one of us would say, "Remember last Christmas when…" or, "At your last birthday we…" A family without memories is not a family.

That first year we spent a good deal of time sharing past personal experiences. Our three stories became the woven braid that framed this fragile new family mandala. During our second year the awareness of being an older single parent to these two young daughters inspired me to explore the possibility of adding another person to our family. I became a licensed foster parent with Ramsey County. The first social worker to contact me had two biological sisters whose parents were in the process of terminating their parental rights and the girls needed a home soon.

On August 1, 1978, Terri, age nine and Mary, age six came to live with us. In two years I was the proud mother of four girls. Terri was an overly shy, compliant child who trained herself to do and say the "expected right things" to avoid punishment. Mary was a hyperactive child who learned to get attention from negative behavior.

Terri and Mary spent their early childhood living with one parent, then with the other, then with relatives and back again between parents. The last two years before coming to live with me they were placed in a loving foster home. Through the months as they began to trust me, stories of abuse and neglect flowed easily from Mary followed by denial from Terri who tried to protect her parents. Interior and exterior scars revealed the reality of abuse and neglect. Finally Terri trusted me enough to add to the stories Mary was too young to remember. Would the pain ever go away?

The girls had only a few years to be children in this family before the trauma of adolescence began. Each one walked through her own pain at her own timing. Ruth, Terri and Mary dealt with abuse, neglect and deprivation issues. All four of the girls had to enter their interior painful world of abandonment. Two of the girls were hospitalized for depression. I remember saying to one child, "God will heal you." She shouted back, "Your God will never heal me."

This year of Our Lord, 2008, my daughters' ages will be 41, 40, 40 and 37. The road to healing and recovery is long. I continue to journey with each daughter through her healing process, sometimes side by side, sometimes hand in hand, sometimes at a distance, always trying to discern how to love without being intrusive.

# REGINA

The empty mailbox
bulges with memories
of stamped envelopes
holding the story

of her life.
Once a week a
handwritten letter came
as faithful as dawn.

For forty-three years
two thousand two hundred thirty-six
letters laced me
with home and family.

Seven years later, I catch
myself pulling open the mailbox
door expecting that familiar
envelope tucked between the bills.

Beloved Mother
of Leonard, Elmer and Betty
Died August 1, 1990

# Regina

## Eulogy Read at Her Funeral

### March 18, 1902 – August 1, 1990

Leonard, Elmer and I would like to take this moment to highlight a few outstanding qualities that express who mother has been and will always be to us. She was a faithful woman, loyal to her God, her family, her value system. She expressed this loyalty by her loving actions.

Her loyalty to God meant trusting in His loving plan for her in good times and in painful times. Prayer was always an important part of her daily life. We drew power and strength from her prayers and union with God.

From June 5, 1922 until October 16, 1960 she was faithful to her husband Nicholas.

The three of us could not have had a more faithful mother. Always did she love us and think highly of us. She believed and rejoiced in the decisions we made for our lives. When Leonard was in military service, two or three letters a week was her way of being faithful. I have lived away from my home in Stevens Point since my entrance into the religious community at sixteen and a half years of age and then my ministry in St. Paul at forty-one years of age. For forty-three years I received a letter a week from mom, which adds up to two thousand two hundred thirty-six letters.

She was so proud of her twenty-six grandchildren and forty great grandchildren. A visit from them made her day. Each birthday and Christmas each one received a monetary gift from her. That comes out to an envelope with money every second or third day of the year. The greatest gift she gave her grandchildren and great grandchildren was the quality of her character and her value system. All of us knew we had her love, her respect, and her prayer support.

She was loyal to her friends and her brothers and sisters. This was expressed in letters and phone calls. Years ago I asked her in jest, "Mother did you go to confession this Lent?" She replied, "I have only one sin to confess." My curiosity arose and I asked her, "Which one mom?" She said, "Gossip." Through the years I've come to see that gossip is the wrong word. She has been the storyteller of the family. She would convey from one sibling to another, what was going on in their lives. They would turn to her as the communicator, the link with one another. Because mother played this concerned compassionate role, Aunt Bernie in Nebraska referred to her as her second mother. Mom suffered with those who suffered and rejoiced when things went well with those she knew and loved.

She was loyal to her value system. This involved a life of simplicity, honesty and generosity. Her material things were simple, long lasting, and cared for respectfully. Her honesty was outstanding. We knew who she was and how she thought and felt. She related openly and honestly with everyone. She was always generous and sharing, not from her abundance but from her sustenance.

Mother had an outstanding gift of wit. You could not be ten minutes in her presence without one or more good laughs. Her wit flowed freely and unrehearsed, a gift in good times and a hope in time of pain.

Apart from the incident a few years ago when mother broke her hip and needed assistance recuperating, mother has been a healthy independent woman until her hospitalization in January. She loved her freedom and independence, being in control of her life. To prepare to enter the Kingdom of God she had to once again become dependent, like a child, to give up all control. We had the privilege of being there with her through these painful stages. She had to let go of her good health, her home and possessions, her mobility, her family. Toward the end her body and mind wasted away, until one day she said, "I'm no longer in control, Jesus take me."

Mother had a strong desire to be closer to the Lord. She welcomed people to pray with her. Many of us sang religious songs when we visited her. The union she had with God on earth is now experienced in the fullness of glory. Regina, thank you for who you were to us on earth and who you will be for all eternity. We love you mother, sister, grandmother, great grandmother, aunt, great aunt, and friend.

# My Parents

My parents, Regina Studzinski and Nicholas Osowski were born and raised in two rural townships near Stevens Point, Wisconsin. They were married on June 5, 1922. At the cost of five thousands dollars, dad built our house on 725 Portage Street in Stevens Point. My brothers, Leonard, Elmer and I were born and raised in that house. When I moved to the Twin Cities in 1971, I usually went to visit my mother and brothers every two months.

Often when I went to Point I would drive down Portage Street and linger until I came to house 725 and stop. Last year I was determined to get a look inside the house. I knocked on the door and waited for a long time until a middle-aged man with a not-so-pleasant look on his face opened the door. I said, "I was born in this house." He looked at me and replied, "So?" Then he closed the door and locked it. How could he know he was occupying my treasured castle that held a library of memories.

After my visit at 725 I would go the Guardian Angels Cemetery and kiss the ground where my parents are buried.

Nicholas -- Died October 16, 1960

Regina -- Died August I, 1990

On the ring finger of my right hand I wear my dad's wedding ring. It never leaves my hand. It is engraved with their names and the date of their wedding.

In dad's family there were sixteen children. In mother's family there were twelve children. It is not surprising that we had over one hundred first cousins. We looked forward to seeing some of them each time we visited the farms. When my brothers and I were young we thought Sunday was the best day of the week because we had these ritual traditions: Mass, breakfast, then a trip to our maternal grandparent's farm. Most families would say we had a very untraditional breakfast. With many rural relatives we could have steak and roast during the week, but on Sunday's "hot dogs and buns" were special. My older brother continued this breakfast menu into his adult life.

I lived with dad for only sixteen and a half years. The convent was only a mile from our house. The night mom and dad drove me there, mom said when they left the convent dad was driving way out on the highway before she said, "Nick, where are we going? We've got to go home even if Betty is not there."

At first my dad did not like the idea of me becoming a nun. He said, " You are depriving me of the privilege of walking you down the aisle on your wedding day." As the years went by he was proud to have a daughter for a nun. He was more proud when my religious community encouraged me to pursue two degrees in music education. I played violin, organ, and piano. Dad played the fiddle at Polish weddings. When they came to visit me he usually asked me to play the violin, often he accompanied me with quiet tears.

Dad died at age fifty-nine when I was only thirty years old. I had a short time to know him as an adult because in the convent we had a home visit once every five years. We had happy times as a family, but also sad painful times when dad drank too much. He died in St. Michael's Hospital while awaiting a leg amputation. The day before his death I was present as he received the sacrament of The Anointing of the Sick. While he was saying the Act of Contrition tears fell down his cheeks.

My father and mother and brothers await my entrance into eternal life. I'm not pushing it, I have a lot of living to do if it's God's will. But one day the five of us will sing in harmony as we did driving to the farm on Sunday.

I wouldn't trade a memory or event in my life, happy or sad, because they all make me the person I am today, very blessed, very grateful, and hopefully more compassionate.

Of the many gifts my parents and ancestors have given me two are most outstanding -- my Polish ethnic ancestry and Catholicism, my religious ancestry.

# LEONARD

died. He was one of the few
persons that knew me
from the day I entered earth.

We were as different as poppy seed and sky.
Many folks were not allowed to enter his
black and white world – my gray world was
over-populated.

He was sure God commissioned him to judge and
change everyone according to his standards.
My professor once said, "Love means – to let
appear as is."

He was convinced that his opinion on every
subject was his gift to the universe. I sharpened
my listening skills in his presence.

My brother died – and I miss him.
I love him just the way he was and is.

# WET WORDS

The green oxygen tank stands by his
bed like an hourglass marking
limited days perhaps months in his
ten by sixteen foot sterile universe.

Often he retreats into the memory
log of his seventy-six years. He stays
there until guilt shoots bullets into
his head and heart much like the pellets
of pain he flung on his wife and children.

Apology is the stranger with whom he
never became friends. They know that.
When they come into his room and hear
the tears in his eyes it is enough.

# Leonard

Leonard was five and a half years older than I. As adults I was often reminded how he hated holding me on his lap when we went to a matinee at the theater. The depression years were difficult and mother didn't have to pay for my admittance if big brother held me. I think the movie was a dime, tax a penny, and popcorn a nickel.

Len never liked school. He did like living, sports and companionship. When he was in first grade a family friend recognized this unhappy boy, dressed in a sailor suit, walking by the Wisconsin River when he should have been in school. School work was difficult for him and he was embarrassed reading and speaking because he stuttered. At sixteen he was able to drop out of school and join the Civilian Conservation Corps Camp in Wausau, Wisconsin.

December 7, 1941 Leonard and I were home listening to music when a newsbreak announced, "Japan Attacked Pearl Harbor." He was seventeen at the time and he said, "Betty, I'm going to enlist in the Air Force." World War II and life in the military service was difficult, but very important to him. It was fitting at his funeral to have the Veteran Color Guard present.

On September 9, 1950 Leonard married the most important companion of his life, Jacqueline Peterson. They had six beautiful, wonderful children who live with their families in or near Stevens Point. Len loved and gave individual time and attention playing with his children and decades later with his grandchildren. There was "the fun Len" and "the difficult Len."

The latter was heightened when he used alcohol. He was a very judgmental person and thought everyone should think and believe the way he did. I would say to myself, "God, if you love him totally and unconditionally, then I can too."

Nine years before he died his leg was amputated and one year after that he had a heart attack. These experiences softened him and he was less demanding and more grateful.

The night before he died, Len, Jackie and I sang golden olden songs like "You Are My Sunshine." In the morning when we came to the hospital he said, "I'm going to die today." He died after two o'clock December 28, 1998, in the presence of his wife, children and sister. My brother Elmer was not with us when Leonard died. We called him and he joined us for the farewell.

# Elmer's Letter to Betty

Dear Betty,

You were playing God in the lives of your girls. He wants them to know Him as Father. They must be left to live their lives' experiences.

You've got to learn to leave it in God's hands. By not dwelling on a problem or the circumstances surrounding it, but putting the mind on everything good, everything that is…then leave it in the Lord's hands. It helps to sing, "Turn Your Eyes Upon Jesus"…and the things of this world will grow strangely dim, in the light of His Glory and Grace. We've got to learn to trust God, not only our understanding.

Again, I love you. My prayers will be with you and your family. Praise God for this wonderful opportunity for growth. Praise Him in every circumstance.

In the Lord,
Elmer

# Elmer

My brother Elmer was two years older than I. We almost always had a pleasant relationship except for two days after I was a victim of his merciless pranks. This one is still chilly in my memory.

Tomorrow River ran through my maternal grandparent's farm. It was a fast flowing narrow stream except where it overflowed on low ground onto the field. In the cold of winter that area froze and we enjoyed ice skating there.

One Sunday Elmer went on the ice long before I did. With two long poles he made skate marks on a light blanket of snow that was close to the thin ice where the river was flowing. When I came on the ice he said, "I bet you can't skate as far as I did." Being a tomboy, raised with brothers, I entered into every power struggle to assert my worth. I fell into the icy water and Elmer yelled for my dad and grandpa to help me out.

Elmer was well liked and he had many friends. At seventeen he liked being with girls more than guys. At nineteen he married Lillian Schulist. I do not have many sad convent memories, but not being able, at that time, to attend the weddings of both of my brothers was a deep loss. I was consoled in knowing my prayer for them was answered. Since receiving First Holy Communion at age ten, each succeeding Sunday after receiving Eucharist I prayed for good wives for my brothers. Indeed, Jackie and Lillian were the best. Elmer and Lillian had sixteen children.

When Elmer and Lillian were in their forties they were searching for a deeper spirituality. Through prayer and participation in Charismatic Prayer Meetings they had profound religious experiences that enriched every area of their lives, especially their love for each other.

One weekend while I was visiting my mother and brothers in Stevens Point, I called home about 10:00 pm Saturday evening to see if all was well with the three oldest girls who chose to stay home. They were seventeen and eighteen years old at the time and they were usually very responsible. Ann answered and said there was an out-of-control party at the house. In shock and with concern, my youngest daughter Mary and I got in the car and drove home. In the middle of the next week I received my first and only precious letter from Elmer. He said that he and Lillian were praying for me until 3:00 am. Then he wrote me this letter.

Fourteen years later, Elmer died on October 15, 1999. Lillian died two years later on their fifty-fifth wedding anniversary. Love begun on earth is perpetuated in eternity.

# THIRTY-THREE

Like slow flowing lava
the disease staked its
claim on his body                    Richard.

He was not afraid to die
but he bargained with God for
one more gift of life                    a wife.

My time with him was as sacred
as gazing at Jesus' dying body
without knowing there would be
a resurrection. He was my mentor
teaching me the wisdom of life                    how to die.

He became his father's son
again. They shared stories of
years apart and memories                    buried.

A month before he died
he was cradled in his sister's
home. We passed the days in the
Upper Room consuming
pots of coffee instead of                    wine.

We took turns going into
Richard's presence        lingering
like the last robin leaving its
nest for the                    winter.

He was alone
when his bride came
Death was her name. She
softened his passage through                    darkness
until dawn arrived.

The long eight year night
was surpassed by                    light.

# Richard

My desire to enter a religious community to serve those in need began at the age of twelve when I attended Grade Seven in St. Peter's Catholic School in Stevens Point, Wisconsin. Reading the biography of Damien of Molokai inspired a heroism that enflames me today. Damien, Joseph de Veuster was born in Tremelo, Belgium in 1840. At the age of nineteen he entered the congregation of the Sacred Hearts of Jesus and Mary and was ordained a priest. In 1873 at his request, Damien was sent to a leper colony in Molokai, Hawaii to care for the physical, medical and spiritual needs of the lepers.

I would do nothing less with my life. After high school graduation I would join the Medical Missionary Sisters and devote my life to the care of lepers.

The Sisters of St. Joseph, Third Order of St. Francis, were my teachers in elementary school and in St. Joseph Academy in Stevens Point. By my junior year they convinced me that joining their community and becoming a teacher was equally heroic. December 7, 1946 I entered their community and remained a member for twenty-four years. My first teaching assignment was to second graders in St. Adalbert School in Milwaukee, Wisconsin. I soon realized that teaching was my preferred and innate profession.

When I left the religious community in 1971, I chose to relocate to the Twin Cities. Catholic parishes were beginning to add lay people to their parish staff.

I never forgot my hero, Damien. I didn't know of any lepers in the Twin Cities, but in the mid-eighties through the Archdiocesan St. Paul Minneapolis Aids Ministry, I was privileged to meet and befriend Richard. We met regularly for eighteen months until his death. Richard gifted me profoundly.

This year 2008, Pope Benedict XVI elevated Blessed Damien to sainthood.

# It Was Darker

than
      the
           day
               Jesus

died. Relatives, friends, co-workers left
but we lingered     long     alone
in front of this small lifeless

box. It was like looking at the ruins of
Hiroshima all heaped into one tiny casket
that belonged to

us. Just three days ago a phone call discharged
seven bombs that disintegrated my world:
"Come quickly. I can't wake Bobby up."

        Hours before that I kissed him,
        we rubbed noses,
        squeezed toes in a
        "see you soon" ritual.

Darkness covered the earth for seventy-two hours.
We were escorted to the cemetery gate.
As we left we clung to
           and leaned on
                 each other
until our two black trench
coats became one shroud.

Please don't preach to us
about angels or resurrection.
We buried our family today.

# It Was Darker

In 1984 I was employed by the Church of St. William in Fridley, Minnesota, to coordinate the parish Sacramental Programs. One summer day a couple overwhelmed with grief and loss came to the Parish Office to request a funeral service for their six month old son who died from sudden infant death syndrome. They wanted the service at the mortuary. Our pastor was attending a priest's retreat at Collegeville, Minnesota. I made a phone call to him and he asked me if I would be comfortable doing the funeral service.

It was one of the most difficult services to prepare, yet one of the most privileged experiences to officiate. The couple expressed deep gratitude after the service and burial. They and two other women came up to me and said, "How appropriate it was for a woman to serve in this capacity."

Another woman shared her profound experience. She said, " I have carried such guilt giving up my child through abortion, in not accepting God's forgiveness I have not grieved my great loss until this service. I will seek a Grief Group to help me."

Some of the most sacred moments in our lives are at the saddest and most tragic experiences of our lives.

# DESERT

empty      black
              hole inside
eclipsing   the sun's

rays        the heart
              locked
in storage   some-

place      even sounds
              play mute
dirges     with

in          no one
              populates
her space   she
is
alone

# ALONE

outside
 inside

does it hurt?

not anymore for
I have found
an integrated community
within myself
and now and then
serenity
hangs up the sign
"do not disturb"

# Aloneness

Aloneness was the phantom emotional pain that weaved in and out of my life depending on the closeness of my relationships. Only my very few close friends know that I have had very few close friends throughout my life.

When we were adults my oldest brother Leonard said, "Betty I use to feel sorry for you when we were young. Elmer and I had many friends to play with, but there were very few girls in our neighborhood. I was sad to see you go up and down the sidewalk with your doll and buggy."

From Kindergarten through Grade Six I hung out with several friends from school. In Grade Six I developed my first closest relationship with Dolores, a girl in my class. The relationship was so special that when I entered convent at age sixteen and a half and professed my religious vows, I chose the name Dolores. Each person entering a religious community chose a new name representing a "new calling" or vocation. In the late sixties after Vatican II we acknowledged that our vocation began at baptism so Sister Dolores became Sister Betty.

I loved my years in my religious community. I was blessed with many friends and a few special friends that made me feel loved.

Undoubtedly, my least lonely years were when I began adopting my daughters in 1976. But even then I remember attending the wake of a woman I knew from Guardian Angels Church. I stood near her coffin reflecting on the warm inviting presence that marked her personality. Within the course of fifteen minutes several women came by and I heard four of them say, "She was my best friend." Driving home that night I felt no one will say of me, "She was my best friend."

Why was it so important for me to feel loved exclusively? I don't know, but it was.

I believe that the phantom emotional pain called aloneness, will never really go away until I am One with our Creator. "Are not our hearts restless until they rest in Thee, Oh God." — St. Augustine

# Angels in the Snow

This was the first
winter in eighteen years that I didn't
see "angels in the snow"
playing in my back yard.

Except for their individual faces
imprinted on the wallpaper
and their familiar voices
hanging around the family room
the foster children are all gone.

Lisa was one of the first to come.
We tried to reclaim her lost childhood
that snuffed innocent years
and aged her far beyond
the candles on her birthday cake

        making angels in the fresh snow
        picking the brightest dandelions in spring
        skipping flat stones in quiet lakes
        hiding her with a quilt of dried leaves.

Slowly and seasonally
these new memories
replaced painfully old ones
charred into ashes
that fashioned bricks of new worth –
a foundation for rebirth.

Now Lisa is a mother
and she makes angels with her son.
Perhaps his childhood will happen
in season.

# Foster Parenting

For seventeen years I was a licensed foster parent for Ramsey County, Minnesota. Over the years I had over thirty-five foster children in my first home in North St. Paul and my second home in Maplewood. Because many of the children had been sexually abused I took only girls in my home, with the exception of twins, Matt and Michelle. As a single parent I could care for five children. As one or more of my adopted girls left it didn't take long for a social worker to place another child in my family. I cherish the name, face and personality of each child.

There were times of tears and laughter, temper tantrums and calmness. Sometimes doors were kicked and phones were thrown when a parent failed to come for a promised visit. Often I would invite the girls at breakfast to share their dreams. Sometimes the dreams reflected how long anger, fear and mistrust lingered. My girls and the foster children were privileged to have counseling to address the neglect, abuse, and confusion they experienced in their young lives. To a few of my very close friends I would say," Yes, you get to go with your children to banquets for trophies, I get to go with my children for counseling." I would have it no other way.

Before the electronics explosion we played many board and card games We participated in sports, went to libraries, theaters and plays, hung out in parks and playgrounds, attended seasonal events in the Twin Cities.

I wonder how and where each of these women are today. Lisa was one of my first foster children. We stay connected. I attended the baptism of her youngest daughter three years ago. This spring I went to her oldest daughter's First Communion. Her oldest child Christian will be in Grade six this fall.

# Too Old to Water Ski

I sat by the lake
and fast forwarded
seven decades of water memories

rushing quieting images
of
oceans rivers lakes
pools ponds puddles
splashing
pouring drenching
enveloping
my hot parched
shriveled spirit

I
felt
like
a
hungry needy infant
sucking
overflowing
breasts

# **Water**

I was born June 9, 1930. My first memories of delightful water experiences go back to the age of three or four. On what was predicted to be a hot summer day, my mother brought the washtub from the basement and put it in the sun in the backyard. I filled it with water from the garden hose. When I woke up from my afternoon nap, with a few rubber toys I splashed and played in the warm water for a long time. Dipping my head in the water was not a frightening experience.

My godfather owned a cabin on Little St. Germain Lake in Wisconsin. Several times a year we would join his family for the weekend and fish and fish and fish. I remember my godmother and mother frying fish three meals a day. From the age of nine my father let me row my own boat as long as I stayed near his boat. I think he was tired of having me hook his shirt or jacket trying to cast my fish line far into the water with a cane pole.

I left the convent at age forty-one and adopted my first two children at age forty-six. Then at age forty-eight I adopted two biological, foster sisters. Camping became a favorite family experience. We always camped by water, a swimming pool, a lake, a river and on several occasions an ocean. We advanced luxuriously in camping units starting with a tent for four. One night after a heavy downpour I woke up at four-thirty in the morning and found an angleworm in the puddle by the tent entrance. We went into the car. Ruth had been in America for just one month and this was her first camping experience. She gestured with her hands that I should stop the rain like Jesus did when a storm arose while he was asleep in the boat as his disciples were fishing. No, mama is not Jesus and the rain didn't stop, but that week I bought a tent for eight, years later a pop-up camper, and finally, wow, a mini cruiser.

I was too small to remember what I consider to be my most important water experience, my baptism at the Church of St. Peter in Stevens Point, Wisconsin. That anointing focused, directed and empowered me to live a purposeful life. I was baptized Betty Jane, Betty is a derivative of the name Elizabeth. Later in life as a religious educator I directed parish baptism programs to prepare parents for the meaningful baptism of their child. I had a book on The Religious Meaning of Names and I was in awe when I discovered that Betty, Elizabeth, means "Chosen By God."

# Christmas Night

She
sat
in my lap
and cried.

It was
Christmas night
and parties
were over.

Presents
and empty wrappings
overwhelmed the living room
floor.

She
sat
in my lap
and cried

Christmas
with mom and dad
was in two separate
households.

Grandma's
lap
seemed to hold it
together.

# No Noel

A profound sadness
enshrouds my spirit
and my body is
in a state of inertia.

My ears are numb
to Christmas songs
my eyes are blind
to gifts under the tree.

Peace and good will
to all —

not in my heart
or home
my
family
is
disconnected.

# Christmas Night

My daughter Ruth came to America when she was eight years old. My four daughters declared "Christmas" to be their favorite day in all the year. Christmas 2003 was the first Christmas Ruth and I had not been together. Hallie her daughter was seven years old and it was her first Christmas spent in two households.

# No Noel

My four daughters and their children no longer gather as a family unit, and it's quite possible we never will until eternity. Holidays and holy days are painful for me.

One of my dearest friends said, "Betty, what if the greatest gift you gave them was a happy childhood." These five words help me remain serene, "It is what it is."

# Death

### 1.

what if I don't wake up tomorrow
and death has sucked
the life out of my body
during the night

will soul spirit consciousness memory cease –
will I cease
being
except in the lives
of those on earth
who knew me –

then before I fall asleep
each night
I should sing praises
to the Creator of Life
for the beauty of my life and relationships –
it would have been enough

I should curse the forces
that brought suffering and pain
into the world –
into the lives of those I love –
into my world –
the senselessness of it all

### 2.

what if I
wake up
tomorrow and the Creator
has breathed eternal life
into the whole of my being

### 3.

aha! the rapture

# Reflecting on My Dying and Death

On July 13, 2004 I admitted myself into St. John's Hospital at 5:15 am because of chest pains surrounding my heart. Considering my age and repeated bouts of atrial fibrillation I realized I could be a candidate for a stroke or heart attack.

Now as I lie in a hospital bed waiting for test results, I reflect on this question. What are my feelings about incapacitation, dying and death?

My concerns about being incapacitated are two fold: I don't know who would take care of me, and I do not wish to be a burden to anyone. My second concern is that I have minimal financial resources to pay for expenses. Responding to both of these concerns I need to believe a Nursing Home and Medicare will be my angels, and I trust in God's unconditional care and love for me. I do not fear dying and afterlife. I believe in eternal life with God and those who preceded me in death. I know this "no fear" will be tested if my dying process lingers.

I have lived a long and relatively happy life. I am grateful for my family of origin. I am grateful for a full, youthful teenage life and twenty-four wonderful years in a religious community — and teaching in Catholic schools. I celebrate the joy and challenge of being parent to Mary, Terri, Ann and Ruth, and the privilege of fostering over thirty-five children through a seventeen-year period. I cherish the joy of being grandmother to Shadia, Jeremy, Hallie, Joshua, Jacob, Shelly and Melanie.

Currently I find joy in serving mentally challenged adults and I am enriched by a  growing faith life fostered by special friends, Faith Sharing Groups and Church Communities.

Of course there have been days, periods, and stages of pain and sorrow, fear and anger, dreams and hopes unfulfilled. But in my seventy-four years, I am grateful for God's unbounded grace and for my overall positive attitude and trust in troublesome and emotional times. If I die before my daughters are in a friendly and loving relationship with me and each other, I am sorry for the sadness, pain or guilt they may have depending on the degree they have bonded with each other and with me. Of all I have been or done in my life, being a parent and grandmother has fulfilled me the most as a woman.

How can I have any regrets about dying after this full life?

# When My Daughter

stopped talking
to me I thought
the pain would break my heart
like a quaking
splits open a piece
of solid earth

decades of loving
caring attending
seemed swallowed up
and lost
in the dark crevice
never to be retrieved

shock stunned
my most joyful spirit
and monsters
of hurt and anger
plagued my waking hours
until

Kahlil Gibran's words
"Your children are
not your children.
They are the sons
and daughters of Life's
longing for itself"
set me free
then

alone
in a forsaken alley
I gave birth
and cut
the cord with
my file in
my purse

# Too Ironic

to
mourn
a
living
dead
daughter
I
pace
between
memories
and
mailbox
for
a
vestige
of
her
presence
and
listen
for
a
sound
to
re-connect

# When My Daughter

There are joys and sorrows in each stage of life. June 9, 2008 was my seventy-eighth birthday. These past eight years have been the most sorrowful period of my life in the history of my braided family because we are no longer connected. When my three oldest girls were ten and eleven, I taught them two card games, pinochle and 500. We played cards often and for long periods of time. Mary was three years younger and somehow we never did teach her those games because we always had a four-some. One or two years before my seventieth birthday, two of my daughters had head-on conflicts and they stopped speaking with each other, resultantly, the five of us no longer gathered together.

I told each daughter that I wanted one, and only one gift for my seventieth birthday, to gather together and play cards. I thought if we played cards they would remember the endless hours of fun we shared and it would ease the tension. We did gather along with the grandchildren but in less than an hour tension resumed and Terri and her daughters left. That was the last time we have been together as a family unit.

I haven't seen Terri for over six years. I have made overtures to connect but received no response. Ruth has refused contact with me for five years. We exchange words on occasion as we meet for the grandchildren's school events. I sit by her and talk with her like I always did when we were connected.

Will I ever get my seventieth birthday gift? One of my co-workers said recently, "Betty, can't you just reconcile?" It would be easier if something precipitated the situation and, "I'm sorry, please forgive me," might heal the separation.

With God's help I have moved through the sorrow, grief, and anger, into serenity. "It Is What It Is" is my white flag of surrender to situations that I have no power to change. My prayer and hope for each of my daughters is for their happiness and for spirituality in their lives.

# Belonging

I forgive you
for walking away.

You were only eight
when you came
to live with me.

We were deprived of
important bonding years —
now you search elsewhere
for love.

I can't and won't
run after you.

Perhaps
when you find
belonging out there
you will know
it began in here —
my heart
and home.

# Desire

I wanted
to get close
to you. You

guarded the entrance
into the depths of
your pain where even
a cry or falling
tear would
transgress
the sacredness of
that dark silence.

I wanted
to get close
to you. You

guarded the entrance
into your fear that
life would pass you by
before you mattered to
anyone.

Perhaps
someday
you will know

you matter and inhabit
my desire.

# Beloved Daughters

I am seventy-five years old and there is so much I want to offer you about aging joyfully, and celebrating life, until I take my last breath. I am sorry for you that you have cut yourself off from me. I am sorry for you that you are not around when I can show you how to age serenely, love unconditionally, and find fulfillment in "being" when there is less "doing."

Terri, Ruth, and Ann for a brief period of time:

No, it wasn't ok. for you to ignore me. It was seriously wrong, unconscionable, hurtful and disrespectful. God said, "Honor your father and your mother." He didn't say honor your mother if she is perfect.

We didn't pick our birth parents and if we were adopted as children, we didn't pick our adoptive parents. It is a legal and lawful responsible relationship. It implies responsibilities on the part of the parent and the daughter.

I choose to forgive you, but I will never forget. I have never not been there for you as much as I was capable, and as much as I knew how, except when you wouldn't let me.

I will always love you. I believe that wholesome relationships begun on earth are boundlessly perfect in eternity. My prayers are always for your happiness.

— Mom

# Legacy

His trigger finger
crazed with madness disease
riveted death empowering bullets
into young flesh.
Why did Barney and Sesame Street
legos and trucks
fail to diffuse a malignant bomb
growing inside this small boy?
Collected wisdom
of counselors psychiatrists parents and teachers
emoted impotence
trying to tap the core of this boy's rage –

these children killing children.

    Unsolved mysteries
    leave no legacy
    for the next generation.

# I Was in Prison and You Came To Visit Me

As a child in a Catholic Elementary School I remember reading Chapter 25, from the Book of Matthew. Jesus said, "I was in prison and you visited me…what you did for one of my least brothers and sisters you did for me." Why would I want to do that? To visit those in prison sounded too scary for me.

When I was in my thirties my nephew Jim was incarcerated. I always liked Jim, he had a gentle spirit whenever I was with him. Of course I visited him. He spent many years in various prisons until he was diagnosed with schizophrenia and was helped by medication and psychological counseling.

In 1968 and 1969 I was employed as Coordinator of Religious Education in Resurrection Parish in Green Bay, Wisconsin. A group of Sisters living in the parish convent went once a month to Waupon Prison for Mass. After the scriptures were read we gathered in small groups with the inmates and shared how those readings applied to our lives. I was inspired by the men who truly knew themselves, and trusted in God's forgiveness for the serious mistakes they made that hurt their families and their victims.

In the 1970's the Charismatic Renewal in the Catholic Church and elsewhere was drawing people into a spirituality of developing a personal relationship with God. Often I participated in a weekly prayer meeting at St. Peter's Parish in North St. Paul. A group of us began going to Charismatic Prayer Meetings at Stillwater Prison in Bayport, Minnesota. Once again I was in awe at how vulnerable the men were in admitting deep sorrow for ruining their lives and the lives of others, with the hope they can reconcile with those they hurt.

For the past four years I have been going once a week to a Regional Correctional Center in Roseville, Minnesota. I facilitate sessions on *Forgiveness and Self Acceptance, My Spiritual Journey From*

*Birth Until Now*, and I lead seasonal prayer services. The women realize the value of having spirituality in their lives to give them the help they need to direct their lives meaningfully. I often tell them, "This is my favorite morning of the week."

Why wouldn't I visit those in prison?

# Karla

She sat on the floor
     drumming the fingers of her right hand
     on the hardwood floor
     like a centipede in motion.

Her left hand reached for a cloth doll.
Ten fingers raced the limbs
     pounding face and mouth
     threshing her prey
     searching desperately

Searching for voice
     in fabric and stuffing

     a voice to

Unlock the child
     Silent and hidden
     like a moth arrested in a cocoon

Frozen forever

# The Mentally Challenged

My two brothers and their wives gifted me with twenty-two nephews and nieces. If I had to pick the one to whom I am most attracted it would be Pamela. This beautiful happy child, now in the forties of her life, has Down syndrome. She speaks almost incessantly with her smiles, laughs, wide searching eyes and hugs. When my brother Elmer died and his wife Lillian had macular degeneration, Anita, my niece, and Pamela's sister took her to live with her family in Chicago. On occasion when I see Pamela her face lights up with memories. She is almost always joyful but she also shows deep sorrow when she remembers or sees pictures of her deceased parents.

While I was a licensed foster parent for Ramsey County for seventeen years, I also worked for Nekton Agency doing respite care for disabled young adult women who lived with their parents. I would take them into my home one weekend a month. Always there was a special event or activity in the Twin Cites in which we could participate.

For over two years I went one night a week into Karla's home. Karla had Rett syndrome and she was unable to walk or speak. During that evening her mother could have an undisturbed night of sleep because I slept in Karla's room with her. Sometimes she had seizures and I was able to monitor her.

Mentor Network incorporated Nekton Agency. For the past ten years I have been the sole staff person for the weekend night shift in one of their group homes. In our home there are six residents. Their disabilities include severe mental retardation, autism, Down syndrome, blindness and partial trisomy 13. Five of the residents are none verbal, Leah has a collection of selected phrases like, "gotta go to work -- how do you feel?" She is a savant and can play the organ and sing many songs.

As I am parking my car in front of the home, John age thirty-one, is already looking out the window for my car. Wearing his under-shirt and boxers he runs to the door, holds it open for me and gives me a handshake with the tips of his fingers briskly sweeping my fingers. The other five residents are in their bedrooms. John hangs around with me for about an hour before he goes downstairs to his bedroom. Friday and Saturday night after watching television in his room, Fred age fifty, comes downstairs to talk with me. I talk, he nods accordingly, and is very aware of what I am saying. I talk about tomorrow's weather, the calendar, the season and holidays, special events, and his staff notes from his work. On Sunday nights Fred goes to bed early because I wake him up at 4:30 am for his bath. His bus arrives at 7:30 am to take him to his work program. Fred operates on only one rhythm, adagio or slow, and it takes three hours before he is ready for work.

Henri Nouwen was one of the most popular spiritual writers in the world. Even though he had friendships and notoriety, he had a restless unsettled spirit and was always looking for a place where he belonged, a home. Before his death he found that home in the L'Arche Daybreak Community in Richmond Hill, Ontario, a home for permanent, intellectually handicapped residents. In some ways I have felt a spiritual symbiotic relationship with Henri Nouwen. Every weekend when I go to work at the group home I feel like, "I'm not going to work, I'm going to one of my families."

# My Addiction

One of my dear friends asked me, "Betty, why would you choose to share information about your addiction in your book?" I said I would be remiss if I didn't. Being a compulsive gambler over a period of time, understanding my addiction, and being in recovery is significant to me.

Every Friday night at the Gamblers Anonymous meeting in Burnsville, MN the over fifty participants begin our meeting by introducing ourselves saying, "I'm Betty, I am a compulsive gambler." I have been in recovery since April, 2003. As I look back at my personal and family history I believe my addiction was manifested at age five. The corner candy store in Stevens Point, Wisconsin had a stand up board in which one dropped a penny at the slot on the top and nails directed the coin to the finish line that said, five cents, ten cents, twenty-five cents, and many zeros. As much as I liked candy, often when I had a dime I converted it to ten pennies and played the game of chance. More often I left the store without my dime and without the candy bar. As children we played cards for recreation, and frequently, for pennies, nickels and dimes.

When casinos opened in the suburbs of the Twin Cities it was not surprising that in the mid-ninety's I began going once a week for several hours. I justified what in the beginning appeared to me to be my recreation. I led a simple life style mostly in service to others. My children and foster children were gone. I was not accountable to anyone for my time and money. I was not hurting anyone. But when I crossed that invisible line from recreation to addiction, I realized how much I was hurting myself. Until I understood addiction I harbored guilt for being too weak, and not having enough will-power to refrain from gambling.

During my period of gambling I continued to seek spiritual growth through prayer, meditation, Eucharist, and other spiritual exercises. In all my work and relationships I always asked for God's help, but I did not invite God into my world of gambling. I thought I could win all by myself. In reality I was a loser all by myself. While I grieved the loss of my financial savings, I grieved even more the loss of "the gift of time" spent futilely, selfishly and purposelessly.

Through the wisdom and guidance of the Twelve Step Program I admitted my powerlessness over gambling and came to believe that God and not my will-power could restore me to a normal way of thinking and acting. Daily I turn my will over to God through the Gamblers Anonymous fellowship and the Twelve Step Program and I am empowered day by day.

This experience in my life has given me a peek into the door hole of the world of addictions that affect so many people all over the world. I know the pain, hopelessness and despair the addicts and their families and loved ones experience. I know the wisdom, healing and growth that can come through Gamblers Anonymous fellowship, the Twelve Step Program and the companionship of a Sponsor.

Hopefully I am a better and more compassionate person because of this ongoing experience and recovery. Two well know prayers that are very significant to me are, The Lord's Prayer and The Serenity Prayer.

GOD GRANT ME THE

SERENITY TO ACCEPT THE

THINGS I CANNOT CHANGE,

COURAGE TO CHANGE THE

THINGS I CAN, AND THE

WISDOM TO KNOW THE

DIFFERENCE.

# Twenty-Four Memorable Years

For twenty-four years I have been privileged and blessed to be a Sister of St. Joseph, Third Order of St. Francis at the St. Joseph Motherhouse in Stevens Point, Wisconsin. Our community living and life style was spiritually, psychologically, intellectually, and physically wholesome. If I did not live so far away from Stevens Point I would continue to be an associate with the community. My greatest loss in leaving was not being able to stay connected with long time friends, my Sisters in Christ.

I am deeply indebted for all the opportunities for spiritual growth, and for the education given to me by the community. While I had a Bachelor's and Master's Degree in Music Education, I was also gifted with a Master's Degree in Religious Studies which enabled me, when I left the community, to be employed as Coordinator of Religious Education in parishes in the Twin Cities.

Early in my religious life because of large enrollment in Catholic Schools Sisters began teaching while they were working on their education degree taking courses on Saturdays and in summer. The leadership of the community sent us to the school and parish that most suited their needs and our education and gifts. In August we found out what "our mission," convent and place of appointment would be for the new school year. Obviously, the discernment process is quite different now.

The following list is my itinerary of places where I lived and the ministry in which I was involved.

| | | |
|---|---|---|
| St. Joseph Motherhouse<br>South Bend, Indiana | 1947-1949 | Novitiate |
| St. Adalbert Parish<br>Milwaukee, Wisconsin | 1949-1956 | Teacher<br>Student |

| | | |
|---|---|---|
| Alverno College<br>Milwaukee, Wisconsin | 1954-1957<br>Res. Blessed Sacrament Parish | Student |
| St. Stanislaus Parish<br>Stevens Point, Wisconsin | 1957-1961 | Teacher<br>Organist |
| Assumption BVM Parish<br>Pulaski, Wisconsin | 1961-1963 | Teacher<br>Organist |
| Lourdes High School<br>Chicago, Illinois | 1963-1964 | Teacher |
| Maria High School<br>Stevens Point, Wis. | 1964-1968 | Teacher |
| Wisconsin State University<br>La Crosse, Wisconsin | 1968-1969 | Newman Ministry<br>Res. Aquinas Convent |
| Resurrection Parish<br>Green Bay, Wisconsin | 1969-1971 | Coordinator of<br>Religious Ed. |

One of my memorable teaching years was in Pulaski, Wisconsin, when I had a combined seventh and eighth grade class of fifty students. ADHD had not been invented yet.

It was exciting to be in the Catholic Church and in a religious community during and after the Second Vatican Council, 1962-1965. Inspired documents and directives brought many needed changes within the Church and defined more clearly our mission in and to the world.

While I was fulfilled in my vocation of being a nun, as a woman I always had a desire to be a mother and to adopt older orphaned children. This desire intensified in my late thirties and I went through a discernment process. In leaving the convent I would not be living community life in accordance with the vows of poverty, chastity and obedience. I would be living the vowed life of my baptism, trying "to be the Christ the world will see until He comes again."*

With God's grace, my parish of worship, faith sharing groups and the support of wonderful friends, I continue to try to live a simple prayerful life as proclaimed by the Prophet Micah: "To act justly, love tenderly and walk humbly with your God."

** From the Song, "The Christ The World Will See," Composer, John D. Becker, ©1988*

# And More

Since leaving my community and coming to the Twin Cities in 1971 I have had the joy of being on staff at these three parishes in the Archdiocese.

| Parish | Position |
| --- | --- |
| St. Peter's Parish<br>North St. Paul, MN | Coordinator of Religious Education<br>1971 –1984 |
| St. William's Parish | Sacramental Coordinator<br>Faith Formation Grades 1 – 6<br>1984 – 1990 |
| Guardian Angels Parish | Volunteer Co-Facilitator, RCIA<br>1990 – 1998<br>Coordinator of First Eucharist and<br>First Reconciliation 1998 – 2004 |

The mission and ministry in each parish enriched me spiritually and wholesomely. I carry in my heart and memory the names and faces of many members of each parish staff and parishioners with whom I interacted. We broke open the Word, we shared Eucharist, and we reached out to serve others. Community is as community does.

Presently, as a volunteer, I am involved in my parish of worship, Guardian Angels. I am a Eucharistic and Welcoming minister. I am active in the Beyond Just Faith Program and I am a Co-facilitator in the Engaging Spirituality Program.

In the wider community I am a Guardian ad Litem for children in Ramsey County, Minnesota. With my seventeen years of experience as a foster parent, I continue to choose to work with children and families struggling with multiple issues that warrant them protection and services from Ramsey County.

Each week I look forward to interacting with the women who choose to participate in the sessions I facilitate at the Regional Correction Center, Volunteers of America, in Roseville, MN.

Through the years I have been mentored and inspired by the fellowship of two important small faith sharing groups to which I belong. In 1973 I became a member of a CYC group, Christian Living Community. We gathered bi-weekly for more than a decade, then we met monthly, and presently we meet two to four times a year. The other group is a women's faith sharing group that has been meeting monthly since 1991. At our last meeting when I was telling them about this book, they teasingly insisted that I should name them. Each month one of our members hosts the meeting and determines the topic we will discuss. Then we share what has been happening in our lives. I call this part of our meeting, the gospel according to Corrine, Pat, Jean, Mary Jo, Kathy, and Betty. The word gospel means "good news" and it continues to be seen, heard, and lived by Jesus' disciples today. I have been nurtured for thirty-five years with the CLC group and seventeen years with my women's group.

# The Dragon

gnawed at my brain
and began to consume my
self-esteem until I almost
succumbed.

Did I fail at my most
challenging task in life
parenting? I

remembered
replayed
reenacted
the scenarios where my
daughter felt I let her
down.

It was at those times
I had to remove myself
so she could
own her own becoming.

The dragon hung around
a few more years
then died of starvation.

# A Braided Family Unstrung

In my childhood and adulthood I was surrounded with the support and companionship of family, extended family, and other meaningful relationships. As a single parent who adopted older orphaned children, I wanted them to also have a support system. When my four daughters were young we went bi-monthly to Stevens Point, Wisconsin to connect with their grandmother, aunts, uncles and cousins.

It was my expectation and hope that when my daughters left my home, we would gather most Sundays for brunch and family support. With the rhythm and flow of each of my daughter's young family life, it didn't happen. We did gather for holy days and some holidays and birthdays. Through the years, divorces and problems arose in some of their lives, and conflicts between two of my daughters resulted in separation and the disintegration of our family connectedness. This once braided family became unstrung.

## Ruth

My oldest daughter Ruth is the proud mother of Hallie age thirteen, Joshua age eleven, and Jacob age ten. Ruth and Jim, the father of their children are divorced. They co-parent their children lovingly and responsibly. While it is difficult for the children to have their parents live in two households, they know that both parents make good decisions for their happiness, welfare, education, sports and other school and community activities.

When friends see me with my grandchildren I sometimes say," Don't my Korean grandchildren look like me?" The ensued response usually is, "Why yes, of course Betty." I cherish each opportunity to spend time with Hallie, Joshua and Jacob. For many years,

Ruth and I enjoyed a strong relationship. For many painful reasons, our relationship is now strained. Hopefully one day we will re-connect on a regular basis.

# **Ann**

Ann is seven months younger than Ruth. It has always been important for her to pursue education. She graduated from St. Thomas University with a Bachelor's and Master's Degree in Business Communication. What was more important to her than education was to be happily married and to have children. She was married to Peter for seven years, but it seemed best for both of them to terminate the marriage. Now, at forty, Ann wonders if she will ever have the two most important values she desires.

Almost three years ago Ann chose not to see me or talk to me. Then I had my three oldest daughters disconnected from me and each other. Our braided family separated into individual strands. I thought my heart would break with pain; instead I journaled and wrote pain poems.

After two years of silence and absence Ann and I re-connected. Our time together was awkward for awhile. I waited for about two months before I asked her, "May I share with you the emotions I had during our separation?" She said, "Yes." I had no intention of speaking negatively to her or blaming her; I just wanted to share my pain. I said, "Ann, I was deeply sad and I experienced profound grief. In and out of these two emotions I had anger but it has always been difficult for me to harbor anger. Eventually I said to myself "Betty, I don't think this is so much about you as it is about Ann." She stopped me and said, "You are right mom. It had nothing to do with you at all."

She went on to say she needed time alone to face the reality of possibly another disappointment in her life; the most important one. "Will I be happily married? Will I be a mother?" Our relationship is at a deeper level than it ever was in our thirty-four year relationship.

# Terri

Terri and I had the shortest time living together as mother
and daughter. She was almost ten years old when she came, and at
seventeen she began pulling away when she experienced her first
love. Michael was her world. They moved in together. They each
had a lot of pain in their childhood and as adults they went through
difficult struggles alone and together. They lived together for ten
years before they married. Their greatest treasures are their children,
Shelly age twenty, and Melanie almost seventeen. When their girls
were young we gathered together with my other daughters and their
children. We celebrated holy days, some holidays and special events.
Since Terri pulled away I miss her and Michael and my grandchildren,
Shelly and Melanie. I respectfully wait for her overture to re-connect
and I periodically send her a note hoping this will happen.

# Mary

My daughter Mary was thirty-seven on October 15, 2008.
But every once in awhile I remind her she is stuck with the title "baby
of the family." I don't know if this is "a Polish thing" but even when I
was a nun in the black habit my mother introduced me by that title,
"This is Betty, Sister Dolores, our baby." Many of my friends describe
Mary in these words, "She is so sweet." School was difficult for Mary
so her High School graduation was a welcome event.

At nineteen Mary met Ahmad, a Palestinian Arab from the
country of Jordan. He came to America for his education and he de-
cided to stay here. In the first year of their relationship Mary enjoyed
her first trip abroad meeting Ahmad's family and relatives that reside
in Jordan. They welcomed her into their family. Mary and Ahmad mar-
ried, and several years later my beautiful granddaughter Shadia was
born. Shadia was fourteen in January, 2008. After almost eight years
of marriage Mary divorced Ahmad. My daughters and I expressed
sadness over this decision, but we continued to offer her our support.
Mary and Shadia have a close relationship. The highlight of Mary's life
is spending time with Shadia.

Two years after the divorce Ahmad went to Jordan for
a wife, a step mother for Shadia. He married a wonderful woman
named Rola. They live in Chanhassen, Minnesota. Ahmad and Rola
are raising Shadia; they also have two children Karam age seven, and

Melak age three. Of course, I'm their grandmother also. They speak English when I'm there, but all five of them speak Arabic fluently.

I am proud to have a Muslim granddaughter. I usually call her the day before the Ramadan fast to encourage her in this sacred time. Each year I say to myself, "Maybe I'll do the Ramadan fast this year to be emotionally and spiritually connected with Shadia and her family. But then I say, well, maybe next year." And Shadia's been fasting since she was five years old? Wow!

## From Sadness to Serenity

The turning point for me with the separation of my daughters was when I stopped dwelling on my pain as a mother, and began reflecting on the pain each daughter had in her early life, and now in her present situation.

I could never think about not seeing and talking to my mother. Even now I continue to talk to each person in my family, though they are in eternity. I may never know the reasons and factors that precipitated the separation, but it must feel empty and painful to not feel one has a mother.

## Journal Entry, May 10, 2005

I need to forget my pain and their lack of appreciation for me as their adoptive mother.

How can I best be their mother in this time of separation?

What positive move could I or should I make in their lives?

Motherhood is forever!

# Parents

AWAITING CONTACT
FROM A SEEMINGLY ESTRANGED
CHILD
WHO CUT THE SECOND CORD,
CONTROL

DON'T CRY!

DANCE
ON THE SIDELINES
WAITING FOR THE NEXT CURTAIN TO
OPEN
ON A SEEMINGLY MARVELOUS
PERFORMANCE.

August, 2008

Dear Mom,

After you read your book to me I haven't stopped thinking about what you are going through. I am so lucky to have you in my life. I go to bed with tears in my eyes thinking about you. I feel I am lucky to have you as a mother and a friend. I thank God every day that you have been there for me for thirty years, and I couldn't have done it without you. You will always be my mother. I consider you my only mother in spite of everything I went through. If it hadn't been for you I wouldn't be where I am today in my life. Thank you for everything you have done for me.

Mary

# And Sixteen More

ANGER

AROUSAL

A WAKE

ENIGMA

FOOTLOOSE

JIMMY

MY THIRD FLOOR

OXYMORA

SHE

THE CHANGING OF A DECADE

THE FIRST

THE APPROACH

TOO SOON

TULIPS

WINTER SOLSTICE

WORDS

# Anger

The windows and doors were locked.
A sign on the front porch read,
"Do not enter."

Anger had forced its way
into my home
a year ago.

It consumed my wine,
devoured my hors d'oeuvres
and destroyed all the lights.

For a long time I felt justified
in entertaining this guest —
we were so alike —
it scared me to realize
I could no longer recognize myself.

It was then that I met
forgiveness.

I invited her into
my home.

The sign on the front door now reads,
"Peace to all who enter."

# Arousal

Spring
cracks
ground
unbroken
crocuses
purple
deep
inch
upward
to
sky
blue

leftover
snow
gray
squeezes
moisture
into
earth
brown

Now
folks
cabin
fevered
old
young
between
take
to
nature
seductively

# A Wake

I'm breathing in my coffin
and afraid to raise my head over the
sides for fear of seeing no

 mourners. It's better this way.
My friends stopped calling.
Coffee keeps me awake anyway
and takes the edge off

valium. It's better this way.
My son said seeing me in my
housecoat in the afternoon is as
ridiculous as he wearing a tuxedo in bed.
How would he know – his wife's not

dead. I do miss the little ones.
They say it's no fun with grandpa gone –
like a lock on a toy box.
It's better this way.

I'm breathing in my coffin, and sometimes,
sometimes I feel his breath close to mine.

# Enigma

I've walked
with friends
who opened the door into
their world of depression
> mental illness
> down syndrome
> bulimia
> rape
> addiction.

Self-centered
arrogant
selfish
righteous
intolerant
judgmental
> persons
> won't let me in
> because
> I'm not worthy.

# Footloose

The
empty
prosthesis
stands
at
the
foot
of
the
bed
waiting
for
the
stump
to
bring
it
to
life -
Geppetto
To
Pinocchio.

The
wonder
of
mind
and
science
that
turned
centuries
of
somersaults
of
inventions
enhancing
life
for
this
little
boy.
Run
Pinocchio.
Run.

# Jimmy

My son died first.

Ain't s'posed to be
that way like snow
in June.

Jimmy come back
damn tractor lift crushed
him dead
Jimmy come back

I born you you bury me
Ain't no other way
My heart crushed dead like his head
My son died first.

# My Third Floor

apartment
bids me
to walk out
and ramble among the trees.

I neither have
my feet
on solid ground
nor
soar
in the freedom
of treetop grandeur.

It's the middle
that muddles
my integrity.

I know my source
and my destination –
I get stuck
in
the middle
and
wander.

# Oxymora

A transparent mystique surrounds and distances
this tiny giant. I have once in a while repeatedly
seen him treat his friends like familiar strangers or alien
buddies. At least once a month I meet him bimonthly
for a breakfast dinner. I am repulsively intrigued by
his estranged relationships which he sloughs off
with warm distain and frowning laughter. After
frequent contacts with him I have come to the open
conclusion that it takes many tiny giants and huge
dwarfs to unbalance this yin yang universe.

# She

wraps our blanket
around herself
almost every night
and I wake up shivering like a puppy
left out on the back porch

because she is older
she teases
and corrects me
yet brags
about me before others

I struggle
to find
my identity
apart from her though
I secretly imitate
her roguish ways

she
is the friend
and mirror
I desired for a long time
yet never got –
my sister.

# The Changing of a Decade

after fifty
is a five on the Richter scale.

Shaken ground seems
untrustworthy
like the rip cord on a parachutist's
first jump.

Memories of relationships lost
by death and fault blur
the future with cataractous
vision.

To trust life and love again
is as rashly bold
as extending one's arms
to fly.

But then
today is –
to play
to be
to love agelessly.

# The First

The barren brown earth covered
with last year's dried weeds and
leaves still shivered remembering
long bitter winter months.

Patches of gray snow dumped
by snowplows lingered with
unpopularity near driveways
and intersections.

The terrain was lifeless and
drab except for dots of dull red
berries rejected by the sparrows.
Then,

one ordinary March day like
a kernel of popcorn burst open
from the rising heat, the miracle
of color popped out of the ground.

A purple princess escorted by
green slender linear knights
stretched upward to see her golden
friend ninety-three million miles away.

Her friend smiled
and acknowledged
the first crocus
of the third millennium.

# The Approach

of winter
buttons coats
from
top to bottom
and scrambles
for
scarves mittens and boots

the
sun
hurries
her distant path
before darkness
invades her domain
and the long cold night
is not welcomed
by sun seekers

then
snow
falls
softly through the night
and
its beauty
warms the hearts
of waking winter lovers

# Too Soon

I have been a push-over
for harmony
and clouded my discernment
by doing so.

I forced reconciliation
before its time
and entertained
a pseudo stand-in friend.

She seemed real
for awhile
but intimacy cannot
be feigned;

nor
can
peace
be
one-sided.

# Tulips

Yesterday the tulips in my back
yard opened up.
Brush strokes of pure yellow and velvet red
began to color my black
and white cloister.

I unbolted the windows unlatched the doors
and walked into a
a world of fresh air.

I shed the shroud of shame worn so long
that it almost
left me faceless.

The tulips in my back yard opened up
yesterday.

# Winter Solstice

Darkness
creeps into body and soul
and penetrates intently
hoping to subdue light.

The
night
is
long

then the slow late sun
slithers softly into view
and squeezes

darkness
out
for
awhile.

# Words

```
        WORDS
        O
        R
        D
WORDS                    PAINT


        FEELINGS
        E
        E
        L
        I
        N
        G
FEELINGS                 ON


        PAPER
        A
        P
        E
PAPER                    SO I CAN BE


        HEARD
        E
        A
        R                           O
HEARD                    INSIDE OUT
                                    T
```